Baedd
& Other
Poems

Twm Gwynne

Baedd
& Other
Poems

Twm Gwynne

ISBN: 978-1-7357944-7-1

Ritona

an imprint of RITONA a.s.b.l.

3 Rue de Wormeldange

Rodenbourg, Luxembourg L-6995

Layout and Design: Rhyd Wildermuth

View our catalogue and online journal at

ABEAUTIFULRESISTANCE.ORG

Within

Preface

*We are talking about creating something that
the history of the current order has done a
bang-up job of genociding, mocking, and
parading in front of the slavering consumers
of modern spectacle for their amusement.*
Aragorn!, *Nihilist Animism*

*There are no unsacred places;
There are only sacred places
And desecrated places.*
Wendell Berry, *How to be a Poet*

The long project of rediscovering the sacred and the awe-inspiring in the world is a project of listening, which becomes a project of communication. For me, poetry is an attempt at that communication.

The spirit of civilisation, characterised by a great cultural noise of self-referential, mechanical static, is incapable of listening. The leviathan of our enemies is geared to make a brawl of noise so awful it might be an end to the quiet voices of the earth.

My efforts toward the poetic are an effort at the dialogue central to a changed relationship with the living world. The weapon of civilisation is industry, and the will of industrial society is to standardise and reduce. This is done to transform the many minds and bodies of the world into objects without agency that can be appropriated and traded. I strive to attack these assumptions and behaviours in myself, to instead treat the world as a being, an entity among entities, composed of entities, all with some will and intention mobilising their activity: "everything is full of gods." Civilisation cannot accept sincere relationship with these gods, despite all the world being made of them.

I cannot see myself as a totality; I am comfortable in the sense that my body is simply a community of allied cells, and my mind, my perception of myself, is effectively the crest of the wave of that community. This is a negative thing only if I value a self-image founded on totality.

To paraphrase Aragorn!, we need a new language between ourselves and the world, a language by which the people who try to talk to the world can be recognised and recognise one another. I think a new poetry can begin to fill that role.

I say new poetry because I believe that while poetry once served a meaningful cultural purpose, that purpose is no longer filled by poetry, or by anything. Phenomenon such as "instapoetry" point to a trend by which poetry (among other expressive modes and forms) is made evermore self-indulgent and vapid, increasingly concerned with inter-human communication and obsessed with intensifying that communication through internal signs and self-referential semiotics. Poetry has been degraded to a state of monotonous droning with the general noise of the modern world.

I have struggled to stay honest in my poetry as part of the conversation of the world. What I have written is here, and that is that.

To me, poetry acts as an ecstatic mediation of reality. I have been possessed by images and experiences in a way that demanded expression: the work discussed above, of making poetry more relevant to Western civilisation, stripped out all the value offered by that profoundly honest voice of poetic ecstasy.

Language is only a barrier to the expression of meaning and experience, so if we are to communicate, to have a language, then let that language be a self-conscious one. Let us use language as nothing but a tool, albeit a frequently beautiful one. Let us work toward the co-creation of an aware and unpretentious poetry by which we can point to our experience of moments, knowing in our bones that the pointing poem is not, nor will be, the moment toward which it gestures.

Wendell Berry writes of "little words that come/ out of the silence, like prayers/ prayed back to the one who prays," of a "poem that does not disturb/ the silence from which it came." I have attempted to write poems that came from moments, that point to the moment of communion and engagement that conceived them. May these small sounds exist as offerings to the great silences that inspired them. I pray these poems back to the moments that birthed them, as these moments are the progenitors of all my experience.

I dedicate this collection to my partner. You are my accomplice through life, the wild rose that makes this ruined world beautiful.

Thank you for everything.

The Snake-Tree

Ancient, riven black bark,
Feathered like a great snake
With gentle ferns,
Gnarled like a twisting
Lightning bolt
Is the great pillar.

Rough steps are in the
Beaten clay where
The pounding footfall wears
Away the old soil.

Here the rain would run
In delight as rivers
Down among the roots.

Identities

I must remain conscious
Not to be chained to a symbol
By crystallised identities;
Simple description can never
Encompass everything
Or, anything.

An image cannot hold
Me, being no-thing,
No-thing can mark my borders.

If I am an image
It must be a picture that
Obscures what is depicted,
And muddies any clear water
To avoid reflection.

The Pūkeko

In a waste place of brambles,
Rampant with the wild fennel
And great spines of dead willow,
Coiled about by the stagnation
Of an oily brook,
The lanky pūkeko scrabbles and
Roughly plucks grubs
In the slow gold of an autumn evening.

On Home

My home was lost
In a crossing-place
When dizzy motion made
Warm youth and
Childish myth
Retreat;
No return
By wheels or wings or feet
Can bring me back.

Cactus-Raid

Surging forward deep in the dim
Shadows, knife in hand
And masked, with bloody skin
Owing to the brambled din
Covering-up the ragged land.

Cactus-Song

Turn inwards ever more,
Turn within,
Cry away! from pain and shame
To turn inwards ever more.

Turn to where whirls
The sweet prism and
Sacred soul glimpsed.
Turn to the beetles and the dirt.
Bury in the sweet-grass scent
And shimmering fruit
Gem-like, glistening on the vine
To the slow, luxuriant heat;
The pulsing flower open
To the languid glory of the day.

Twist like a yearning leaf,
Twist and writhe away!
Stretch ever to deny
The slow claim of loam beneath.

This is to say:
I open my lungs to the wide air
And embrace my simple, worldly cares.

Forever

I will not be made to desire
The living death
In sterile simplicity
And bright narrative clarity.

I cyclically choose complex
Muddied pain and rarity
Of thought and experience.
A burning kiss and then
The rot;
I desire the dark mutability
Of mortality
And am compelled to forever reject
Forever.

The Yarrow

Hail the gods that gave to us
The wild and bitter yarrow,
The feather-ferned,
Astringent diviner.
Hail the wound healer, hail painful salve
Hail the silver bloom that
Bursts in pale spray,
War-wound-wort that sprang
Escaping the boar-skull;
Hail the white flower from the underworld.

Untitled

Today I am too tired
To write something profound;
The ignominious work week
Has drowned out all the sounds.

Gone the note of birdsong
And the rough cicada call
Behind the muggy traffic
That works to choke them all.

I have slowly pulled weeds
Until my nails are well worn down
And full of dirt.
Now I want to go home,
But can't.

The Snail

A snail lives in our letterbox
And we, devilish, encourage them
By feeding,
Offering up unwanted letters,
The aggrandising flyers
Of aspiring politicians to
Be humbled by sedate
Digestion.

Dream of the Stone Channel

I.

I wandered by a gorge,
Narrow and jagged,
With a fresh, bright dark
Marking the ragged stone.

I turned down the stumbling way
Of rough rock
To the outcrop
Of a greater chasm;
To the overlook
Where stood
A crude altar hewn
By no hand,
Misted by the soft spray
Of unseen falls.

II.

Many times, I returned
Compelled,
Wearing the way smooth to my step,
Until, at last,
Others followed
And the gorge was trodden
Down, and the walls rose
Around the people-flow.

Terrible!
They were made to loom
With broken faces;
My frightful passage shorn
Of the clean, enfolding form
And fresh night;
Instead I swayed through a throng
In the dusty twilight.

III.

The falling water ceased
In the musty sleeping
From the wake of peace
But the marchers, unabating,
Trampled through the dying place.
The only thing to be done
Was to light the stone
With bloody flame in the bones
And raise the bright nights;
This I did.

On Poets

The poet is a lightning rod
For gods and sights and sound,
To reproduce and make abound
Their message in a word.

The Depths

We are people of deep currents,
Moved by torrents beyond our reach
That still, in a subtle, silent
Moment, those depths will strive to teach.

Bloody Youth

Rise, war-crest,
Above a bloody youth,
Throbbing, proud,
Barbaric, uncouth,
Without grey rest
Below the shroud;
I was a dog among dogs,
A boar among men,
A hunched stone below
Waterfalls in the fen.

Now my war-mind
Is a pulsing, groping,
Goring gyre
Where one thousand hands
Flex at the sky
And the stars
In their bands.

Puawānanga and
Mānuka

I see a slowly stepping sequenced rise
Of buttressed roots,
A fort for youth,
And, climbing hoary age-hoarding trunk,
 the vine
In startling pale bloom,
Ghostly between dark limbs
In the nuanced forest gloom
Where the chipping bark will drip from
 chins
Of those giants who vaguely loom.

This is a generation of pioneers
Who rushed to defend the falling
Naked soils, gouged barren by the years
Under steel abuse, now calling
"Fire to the machines!"

The Land

I am a crest of the great wave
In this golden ocean –
The land is the moving root
That pushes me up.

But, a mushroom warned,
By his changing forms,
"This land that owns will grind your bones,
My boy."
This I was shown.

A View of the Hills

I sit to see the sweetly
Threshing clouds,
Winnowed and caressed by the wistful
Ripples of the land,
The doom-green pine fletching
Stacked like spines,
Like a ragged spire
To the rough and gusting sky.

The Ape

Oh, bold doe-eyed being
With jutting brow
For shutting out
The cold world.

Oh, soul-eyed bark-eater,
Mycelial men
Encircling the tree-root pit
Where the woman,
Holding her child,
Is buried in flowers.

Woe to the ape who makes meaning.

Flowers

Your smooth skin and back
Are soft in a chiaroscuro of
Warm orange light
And dark hair tumbling and tossed.

You are a wild rose rooted in my spine,
That blossomed in my lungs
And bore fruit on my tongue.

As the rambling dog-rose,
As the trailing, tender sweet-pea,
You are my winding, twining flower.

Kinds of Peace

This spacious place between us,
That we have taken to calling a
  "relationship,"
Is so much more than mere relation:
In this void between bodies is
An endlessly creative emptiness,
A gap generative of
Tangling, gentle vines of touch and
Their slow, fervent-glowing blossoms,
Among which we have found
Endless kinds of peace.

Baedd

Raise thy snuffling snout;
Raise, cast about,
Enrage and grunt
O bristled screamer.

Lend me thy narrow
Hating eyes,
Thy goring tusk,
Sharp hooves to
Shred fallow tilth—
And, in thy bristled back,
The matted filth.
Lend me thy panting heat
O warrior soul.

Dw i'n bydd y baedd,
Running down the merchant
And the land-thief.
Rooting through the entrails
I prophesy
No future.

The Cloud

There are clouds hanging in a pale wave,
Shading-out the woolly plain
Below in dark ocean tones
Of spires and softly-mounded swathes.
This landscape is unlike our home,
Yet always poised above and away.

On Suicide

I may be preoccupied with death
Having, as a younger person,
Reached blindly for the cool hand,
For gentle rest.

I have since found my fear of death
And would now, as such, die afraid;
Maybe a self-directed slippage
Out of the world
Would have been a more beautiful,
And more simple,
Culmination of "myself" than this.

Still, all poignancy will pass away,
No precocious prayer could prevent it,
And attempts to validate a life in this way
Are exposed by morning light as replete
With a reified self-abuse; without too
Strong an answer, I no longer find my
life obsolete.

At Journey's End

Two weary folk are winding a way
Through aromatic pines and scorched
Clearings, passing through the glade
And mist to follow the homeward torch.

The staggered hills and lonely vale
Fall away before travelling feet
That turn away from town to hail
The woods, and shy away from chancing
 meet.

The crush of folding ferns and dewy
 grass,
Claggy crags of rain-swept clay
Controlled by soaking gorse as shattered
glass:
On each spine and flower, an ocean plays.

At last, two pass their final distant bend
And huddle in to cosy shelter tend.
At the hearth of she they came to find
Are three folk now, with bloody wine
And ready food between good friends.
Together they passed a merry time;
How sweet their bed, at journey's end.

The Silver Hand

Nodens, Nudd, Nuadha,
Raise the silver hand!
Wake the healer, gird the hunter
By the sea strand.

Hail the Lord of running dogs,
Hastener of pale hounds
With redded ears and redded maw
That track across the widening ground.

That dog is resting by the sea,
With greyly dull salt-matted coat,
Lapping at the salted wound
Of the soul too far remote.

Bright the light on cresting wave,
And dark beneath that questing spray;
The subtle folding waters hold
A soul beyond the blood and bone.

Voices rasp out of the wind,
Shrilly chant the gulls with grim
Knowledge ever harsh and cold
Of how to die and how to hold
The healing role.

This same wind has flattened down
Resistance in the land around;
Every shrub and grass is thrown
Down to the ground, like opened bones.

Rotting wrack and ruined shells
Abound among the broken rocks;
Before me lies the churning well
Bounded round by shattered blocks:
Surging spirit of the wrathful deep,
Bring us back to the dark sleep
Of dripping death to reason dry
And ruin brought on iron lies;
The folding of the flowing mind,
Abiding in the coiling tide,
To unbecome before my vivid eyes

And hold in the cold womb of reborn
 life.
No longer one alone to rise;
Annihilation of this kind.

The breaking sea is rising now,
Driven up by urgent gusts
To roil and thickly turn around
In a fervent hurling rush.

In the furious foam is clear a joy
Adoring the pale sand to toy
And tear away the ragged veil;
Bare the naked rocks but not destroy
Their spires and their piercing edge,
Only wear away in sensuous war
What will forever rise again.

Hail Nudd, hail Nuadha,
Hail the silver hand.
Hail the healer, hail the hunter,
Hail the sea strand.

The Mullein

The flower spikes of mullein
Are unsubtle and fresh
At this time of year,
As bright gold glints glimpsed
From the pale and woolly green
Of soft leaves and pods.
They are proud, pervasive, potent—
Still they are shaded,
Ever-dwarfed
By the grim spires of last year's growth
To which they owe everything.

The Crisis

We came through a little crisis
In the night,
When singing wind and striking rain
Presaged the strange beast of the future;
A rooting boar was in the dark
To announce the tumult of maturation.

Now we have come through without
 conclusions
And a new way of seeing is opened up:
When the dully hanging clouds burst
The tight conflict of our expectations,
All such drabness
Was washed out of the air like smog.

We came through a little crisis
To the morning,
And what a sweet sunrise!

Our hearts were in the beating wings
Of the birds bursting from the mist,
Bursting into golden light and life
Over the green-gold pastures.

Three Gods

I first glimpsed the gods from a distance,
Glowering in their plains beyond the
 girdling hills.
They wore a mighty mist-mantle each
 about his shoulders;
Towering, snow-bound still in summer,
I am set to shiver and tremble before the
 terrors,
The three battling, soul-taking brothers.

O Ruapehu!
Proud in power and furious youth,
I sing of thy smoking slopes
And bitter pinnacles;
I sing of the Pit of Noise,
That lord over the mangled desert
Whose word is roaring law
In this mountain domain.

O Ngāuruhoe!
Embittered enigmatic cone,
Plotting spire of the ruptured domes,
Purple with the spikes of summer
 heather,
You are cold, grim beneath
The golden sun and beyond
The glowing tussock.
I sing with fear of the brother's slave,
Slave-named summoned fire.

O Tongariro!
Low with scars and bloody pits,
Old beyond my soul and years,
Whose jagged form of roughly reddened
 lips
And rushing teeth incite the fear
Of lonely death – many a willing
Sacrifice has walked to doom
Among your rocks returned to killing
Or the pools with ever-greater room
For fresh bones.

I hail thy victory, old god,
The defeat of upstart Taranaki
Which left the flowing scar.
Fear not, old god, the scar
Has softened the warring slopes;
Now when, in mighty age, reaching
To love the sweetly green-gowned
 Pihanga,
You may present a gentler face.

The Implication of Absence

My sense implies my non-sense,
In absence of experience,
As being implies non-being
Or becoming, unbecoming.
The hot mutter of pain in these dense,
 muted limbs
Indicates where my experience moves
In stepping-off, and where it begins,
Implying an absence of limb in absence
 of pain:
This is more terrible.

The Tyranny of the Sun

He beats down on we
Living sacrificial skin drums;
Brilliant, bold orb,
Moulded by the atom thrum.
The climate-changed age
Will cry in pain against
The coming tyranny of the sun.

Recognition of a Picture

I can almost smell the grass from here,
Hear her thousand voices sigh as she
 sways,
Before the breath,
Below the low clouds
Blown down from the hills;
From here, I can taste the falling waters
In the air.

Twm Gwynne

Twm Gwynne is an eco-radical poet and writer, wandering child of misted valleys. More of his writing can be found at his blog:

ydyngwyrdd.wordpress.com.

Ritona

Ritona is an imprint of Ritona a.s.b.l. and Gods&Radicals Press. Named for the Treverii goddess of river crossings, we are a non-profit publishing organisation advocating for plurality, tolerance, and respect for Pagan, Indigenous, and non-industrial ways of being in the world.

Find our online journal and book catalog at *ABEAUTIFULRESISTANCE.ORG*

CPSIA information can be obtained
at www.ICGtesting.com
Printed in the USA
BVHW081219180821
614614BV00014B/1315

9 781735 794471